Betty Foster's
Adapting to Fashion

MACDONALD

CONTENTS

Credits

Editorial manager
Judith Maxwell
Editor
Linda Sonntag
Production
John Moulder
Artists
Ron Hayward Art Group
Photography
Beta Pictures

Published in conjunction with
Thames Television's programme
After Noon Plus edited by
Catherine Freeman.
First published 1980
Fourth Impression 1981
Macdonald Educational Ltd
Holywell House
Worship Street
London EC2A 2EN

©Macdonald Educational Ltd and
Thames Television 1980
Text and patterns © Betty Foster
1980

Printed and bound in
Great Britain by
Morrison & Gibb Ltd,
London and Edinburgh

ISBN 0 356 07180 4

INTRODUCTION

This is not a book about sewing techniques. It is a simple guide to making your own patterns and understanding how they work. It is the result of many years' research in the teaching of both children and adults. Once you have worked through the book you will have learned how to start designing and constructing your own clothes. You will be surprised just how easy it is.

This is a book for all ages and sizes, because everyone follows the same instructions.

Most dressmakers would love to be able to create their own clothes by combining different ideas and perhaps adding a few original touches of their own. Like many others, you may have been put off exploring dress design because it has been presented in a complicated mathematical way, and you were expected to be able to sketch.

You need no longer worry. There are no mathematics in this book and the only ability you need is to be able to do simple jigsaw puzzles. Even if you don't want to make your own patterns it will help you understand the pattern books because you will see how minor changes can create a whole new fashion.

The secret of dressmaking success lies in learning to design patterns in miniature scale before you go on to the full size. On pp 20-21 you will find the starting patterns printed in small scale so that you can trace them off and practise. You will quickly gain confidence in your own ability and once you know how the patterns work you will be ready to make them full size.

To do this you need a Master Pattern. This will be identical in every respect to the miniature, except that it will be correctly fitted to your figure.

In the back of the book you will find a free multi-size pattern. Choose the outline for your size (8-22) and adjust it to fit your body according to the step-by-step instructions starting on p 9.

This is your Master Pattern. It is your key to success and the only pattern you will ever need because it is the correct pattern for your body. You should take a copy of it every time you want to make a different garment and keep the original as a permanent record of your figure.

Now you are ready to adapt your Master Pattern to different styles and this is where your dress designing begins.

Glossary

CB (centre back)
CF (centre front)
The centre back and front are
either placed against a fold or
cut with a seam. This is
indicated on the pattern.

FACINGS
These are shaded dark pink on
the patterns.

DARTS
Shown on the patterns as a 'V'
shape. When darts are closed
out they are indicated with a
pin.

**DARTS ON THE MASTER
PATTERN**
For the purposes of dress
design the darts on the front
pattern are shown to be
touching (A). If you make up
the Master Pattern you should
shorten the side bust dart before
stitching (B).

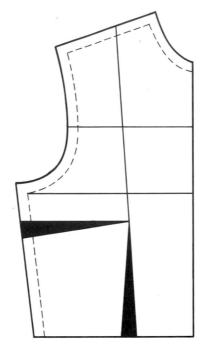

A Darts touching for designing

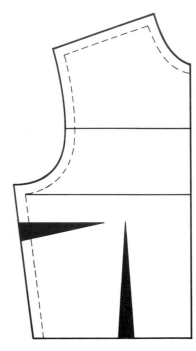

B Darts not touching for
stitching

DRAWING NEW NECKLINES
Practically without exception
all lower necklines need to be
tightened to stop them
'bagging'.
   Fold out a small dart in the
neckline as indicated and open
the side bust dart to allow the
pattern to lie flat. The facing
should be cut after the neckline
has been tightened.
   Note that this method can
also be used to tighten gaping
armholes in sleeveless dresses.

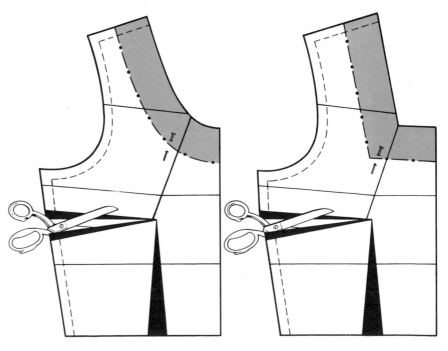

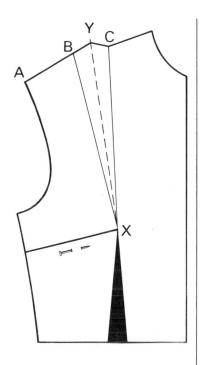

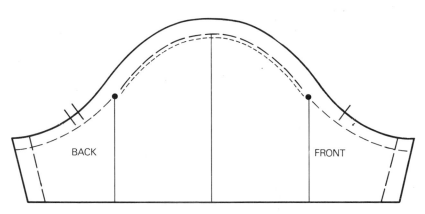

SLEEVE HEAD
The top of the sleeve is called the head. The front and back are marked accordingly and should not be confused. The back is marked with a double notch and the front with a single notch.

GATHERS
These are marked as a broken line with dots at either end. They indicate that the edge should be gathered to fit between the dots.

DRAWING NEW DARTS
In part two of Creating Fashion (p 35) you will see that the side bust dart can be moved into different positions.

When you draw the dart in its new position you must learn not to connect the two edges of the new dart (BX and CX) with a straight line. This could cause trouble at the sewing stage when you need to catch the dart into the seam.

To draw the correct line for the dart mark a line through the centre of the new dart from X to Y. Continue the shoulder line A-B to meet the centre line, then drop the line to point C.

When this dart is stitched out it will lie towards the armhole and can be stitched in with the shoulder seam. This should be noted when you change the angle of the skirt dart on p 32.

SLEEVES WITH CUFFS
It is necessary to make an opening in the back of a cuffed sleeve before the cuff is stitched into place. Follow these instructions for the simplest method.
A Turn a small hem 3 cm (1½ inches) on the back line of the sleeve.
B Stitch the sleeve seam and gather the sleeve bottom to fit cuff.

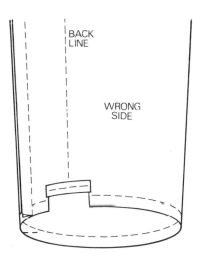

WAISTBANDS AND CUFFS
No patterns are given for waistbands and cuffs as there are several easy methods well illustrated in most sewing books. Curved petersham is recommended for the waist of skirts.

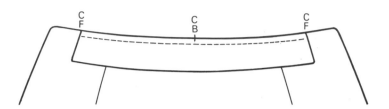

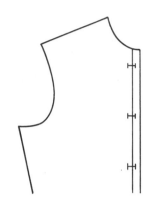

COLLARS

These should always be positioned from the centre back (or front) of a garment before stitching. The simplest way of attaching a collar is to stitch it between the garment and the facing.

BALANCE MARKS OR NOTCHES

Every pattern in this book is shown with the same bust, waist and hip lines as in the Master Pattern. It is this repetition which makes the pattern adaptations easy to understand.

You should notch the edges of the pattern pieces on these lines to make for easy matching up after cutting out.

Be sure to label all your pattern pieces after you have cut them out.

BUTTONHOLES

The size of the buttonhole is obviously determined by the buttons you choose. The buttonholes should overlap the centre front line by about 0.5 cm (¼ inch) to ensure that the fastened button will be in the centre.

GRAIN LINE

It is essential that the pattern pieces are cut from the material in the right direction. Working with the Master Pattern, with its defined vertical and horizontal lines, gives a clear visual guide to this direction.

Blouse buttonholes often go up and down rather than across the garment.

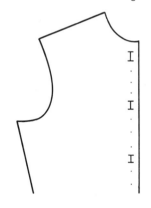

With so many widths of fabric available you need to have a simple fabric planner to help you with the calculations. It is easy enough to make one yourself with a length of paper.

1 Draw the bottom line which represents the folded edge of all fabric widths.
2 Draw lines across the paper in the position shown for different widths of fabric.
3 Mark out the length into yards or metres.
4 When you have made your patterns plan the most economic layout by treating the planner as fabric.

Planning how much fabric to buy

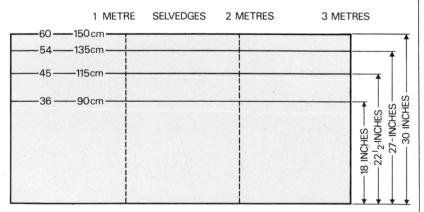

ADAPTING TO FASHION

STEP-BY-STEP PATTERN CORRECTION

The pattern is the most important piece of equipment the dressmaker will ever use. Accomplished sewing techniques and advanced machinery will get you nowhere unless you understand the relationship between the flat pattern pieces and your body.

This book explains in simple terms the mechanics of patterns, and once you have learned how they work, you will be able to construct them for yourself.

The Master Pattern is where the dress designer starts. This is a map of your body and reflects your true measurements. Base it on the free multi-size pattern in the back of this book. Remember no two people are exactly alike and few have standard-sized figures. Your aim is to make a pattern which will **fit you perfectly.**

So be honest with yourself when you take your measurements: don't breathe in or you'll be making your clothes too tight for comfort! Stand normally, which may not be bolt upright, and wear your usual underclothes or a leotard. Look at yourself in the mirror while taking your measurements so that you can see your body's silhouette—and make sure you don't cheat!

Decide whether you are working in inches or centimetres, then fill in your measurements in the boxes provided and at *each step* mark in the alterations you will have to make on your paper pattern, but at this stage **do not cut anything out.**

Shoulder to waist

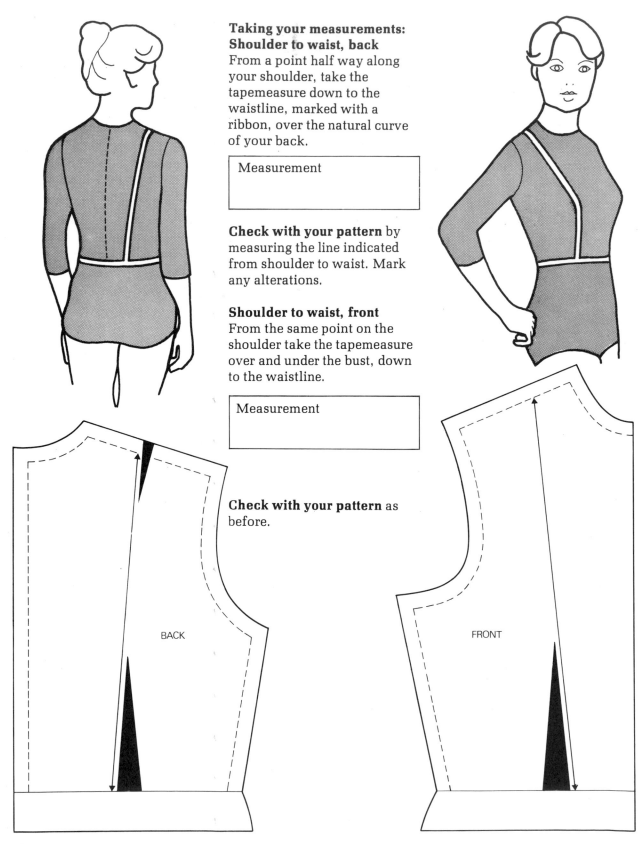

Taking your measurements:
Shoulder to waist, back
From a point half way along your shoulder, take the tapemeasure down to the waistline, marked with a ribbon, over the natural curve of your back.

Measurement

Check with your pattern by measuring the line indicated from shoulder to waist. Mark any alterations.

Shoulder to waist, front
From the same point on the shoulder take the tapemeasure over and under the bust, down to the waistline.

Measurement

Check with your pattern as before.

BACK

FRONT

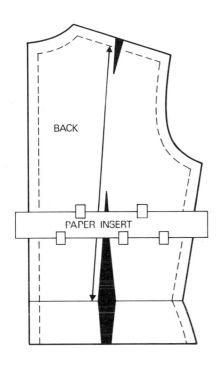

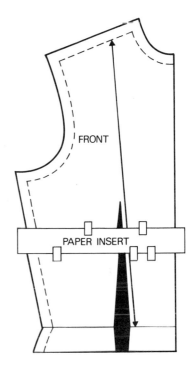

Make your corrections to lengthen or shorten the bodice now, on the line marked 'lengthen or shorten here'. It is unlikely that both back and front will need the same amount of adjustment. For instance, if you have a large bust, you will need more material to cover it, hence the front bodice must be lengthened, whereas your back measurement may be exactly the same as that on the pattern.

Always check your measurements within the stitching line. If you measure to the cutting line, you'll be making your garments too small.

Lengthen by cutting a strip of paper to the required width, cutting the pattern on the line as marked and inserting the strip. Fix it in place with sellotape.

Shorten by taking a tuck in the pattern and folding up the required amount as marked. Fix with sellotape.

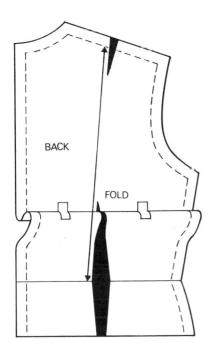

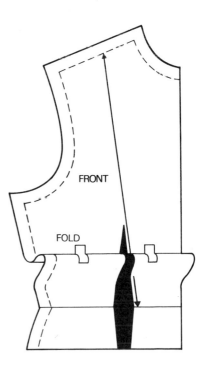

Bust

To all measurements taken around the body 5 cm (2 inches) should be added for ease. This is very important, as even if you like your clothes to fit tightly you must allow yourself room to breathe and move. 5 cm (2 inches) may sound excessive, especially when it comes to measuring the waist, but measure any of your bought clothes and you will see that they are all bigger than you. This is the minimum amount of ease allowed.

Bust + 5 cm (2 inches) ease

Back bust + 2.5 cm (1 inch) ease

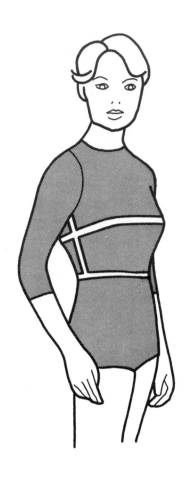

To make sure you have the correct fitting (remember that bust cup sizes vary, and so do the breadth of backs), pin a piece of tape from bustline to waistline under each arm at the side seams. Now measure the front and back halves of your body separately, adding 2.5 cm (1 inch) ease to each measurement.

Put the tapemeasure over the fullest part of your bust, note your measurement and add ease allowance.

Check that front and back measurements add up to your all-round measurement!

Front bust + 2.5 cm (1 inch) ease

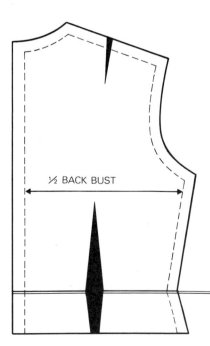

Check with your pattern by measuring across the line as shown. Mark your alterations on the pattern, but cut nothing out, as you have not yet checked the waist.

½ BACK BUST

WAIST LINE

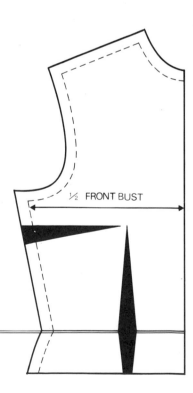

½ FRONT BUST

Waist

Take this measurement (not too tightly!) where your waist tape has settled (see drawing on p 15), and add an ease allowance of 5 cm (2 inches).

Check with your pattern. The waist measurement is normally distributed equally between the front and the back. Check ¼ of your waist measurement (plus ease) following the diagrams.

Note that the measurements **do not** include the darts, as these will be machined out to make the flat fabric take on the shape of your figure.

Mark in your waist measurement on the pattern.

Do not cut the pattern yet. Now you have corrected both bust and waist you can plot your final side seam with an even line as shown.

> Waist + 5 cm (2 inches) ease

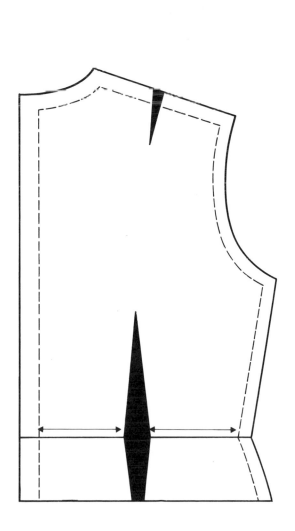
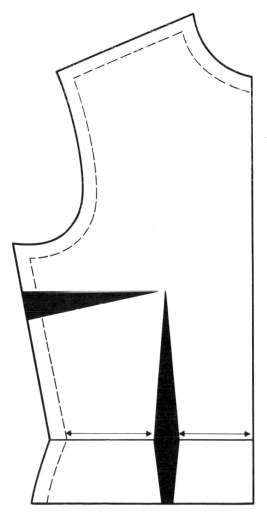

Bust darts

This is a crucial body fitting, and one essential to all dress design, as you will see later on. Get it wrong, and your whole garment will be a disaster. First find out how high your bust is. Measure up from the waist to the point of the bust with a ruler.

Check with your pattern by measuring upwards from waistline as shown. Draw a line across your pattern at the height of the bust.

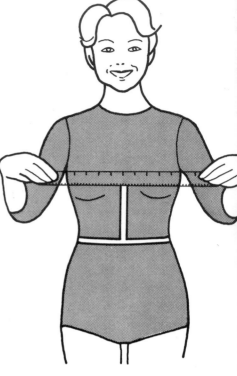

The size of the side bust dart is found by placing front and back bodice patterns side by side with waistlines level. The difference between A and B is the amount that will have to be taken in to make the two sides join up properly. This is your bust dart (C-D). Measure this distance *down* from the bust height line and mark the dart as shown. Complete the waist dart up to the bust point.

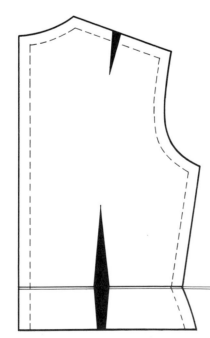

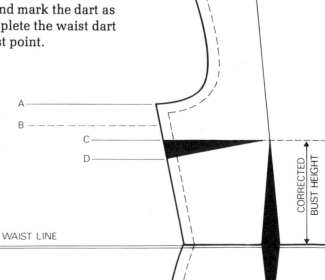

A ———

B – – – –

C ———

D ———

CORRECTED BUST HEIGHT

WAIST LINE

Hips

Take two hip measurements (three for the fuller hip) and add 5 cm (2 inches) ease to each. Check skirt length and add 5 cm (2 inches) for the hem.

Check with your pattern as for waist measurements. Mark your alterations making skirt lines flow smoothly into the waistline. Mark hem length.

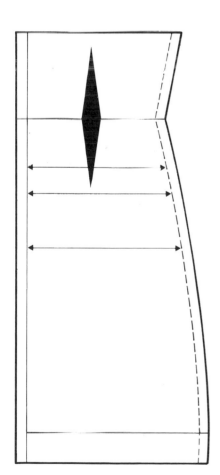

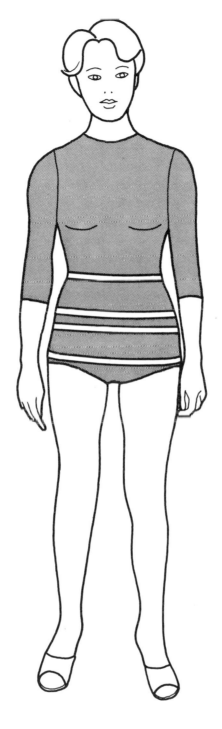

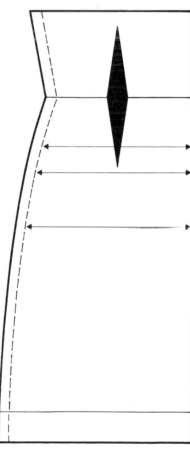

1st hip + 5 cm (2 inches) ease
2nd hip + 5 cm (2 inches) ease
3rd hip + 5 cm (2 inches) ease
Length + 5 cm (2 inches) ease

Back, chest and shoulders

These measurements are all related; after all, you can't have broad shoulders without having a wide back. The chest measurement should be taken at the sleeve level, above where the bust begins to swell; the back measurement at the same level.

Widen shoulders by making an 'L'-shaped cut down from centre to shoulder and out towards armhole. Pull the two pieces apart until the correct measurement is achieved. Stick a piece of paper behind the cut and trim the shoulder line.

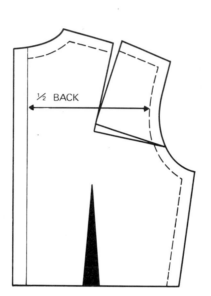

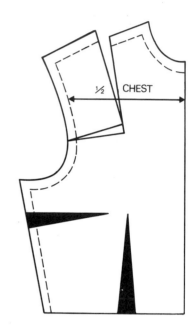

Narrow shoulders by making the same 'L'-shaped cut and folding the pattern in until the correct measurement is achieved. Secure with sellotape and level the shoulder line by patching with paper from behind.

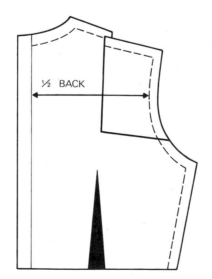

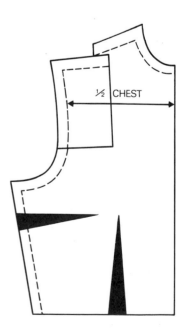

Check with your pattern by measuring along lines as shown.

Sleeve head and armhole

Place back and front bodice pieces together at the shoulder seam and measure the length of the sewing line with a piece of string as shown. Select a sleeve pattern with the sleeve head measuring approximately 5 cm (2 inches) bigger than your armhole to allow the sleeve to be eased into place.

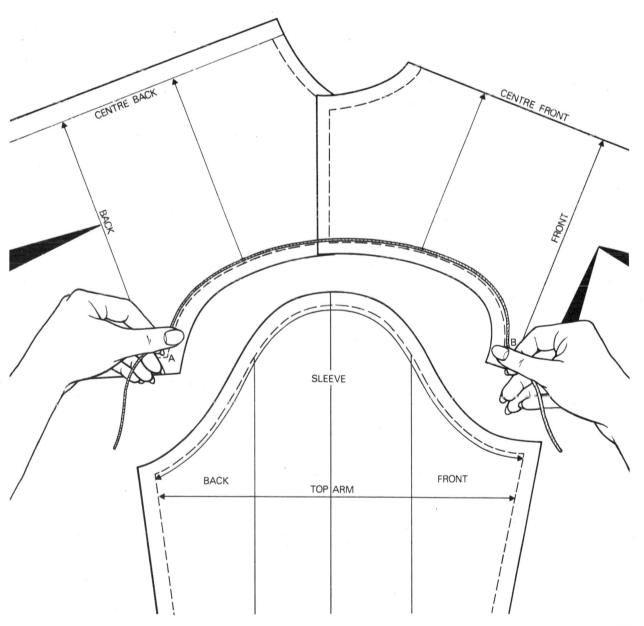

Sleeves

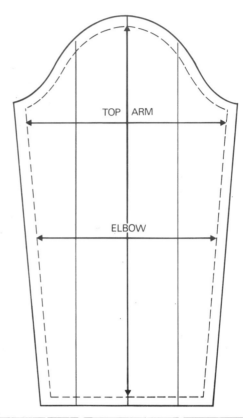

Sleeves
Measure the length of your arm when bent. Add 3.5 cm (1½ inches) ease round the arm where appropriate.

Arm length

Top arm + 3.5 cm (1½ inches) ease

Elbow + 3.5 cm (1½ inches) ease

Check with your pattern, lengthening or shortening at the middle line as for bodice.

Using the Master Pattern

STANDARD SIZES

If you are a standard size you can cut out the dress and sleeve patterns on the outlines indicated.

Size 8 and 10 cut on outline A
Size 12 and 14 cut on outline B
Size 16 and 18 cut on outline C
Size 20 and 22 cut on outline D

If you are sizes 8, 12, 16 or 20 trim 1.5 cm (⅝ inch) from side and sleeve seams.

A seam allowance of 1.5 cm (⅝ inch) is included in the pattern and should be clearly marked after the pattern is cut out.

MISSES SIZE CHART

METRIC

SIZE	8	10	12	14	16	18	20	22
BUST	80	83	87	92	97	102	107	112
WAIST	61	64	67	71	76	81	87	93
HIP	85	88	92	97	102	107	112	117

IMPERIAL

SIZE	8	10	12	14	16	18	20	22
BUST	31½	32½	34	36	38	40	42	44
WAIST	24	25	26½	28	30	32	34	36
HIP	33½	34½	36	38	40	42	44	46

NON-STANDARD SIZES

If you are not a standard size you should follow the instructions below. If you are round-shouldered you should substitute the alternative top back bodice especially designed for round shoulders before proceeding.

1 Select shoulder, neckline and armhole outline most suited to your figure and clearly mark it in coloured crayon, including the seam allowance, to avoid confusion.

2 Follow the instructions starting on p9 to plot your personal measurements step-by-step.
Note you are checking to the stitching lines.

3 Complete the stitching lines at the sides and cut out, remembering to add a seam allowance where necessary.

4 Measure the armhole of your corrected pattern (p17) and select a sleeve pattern to fit. Allow approximately 5 cm (2 inches) ease in the sleeve head. Check the sleeve length. Mark seam allowances on sleeve seams.

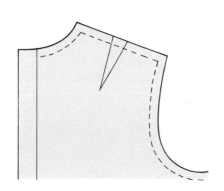
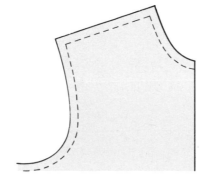

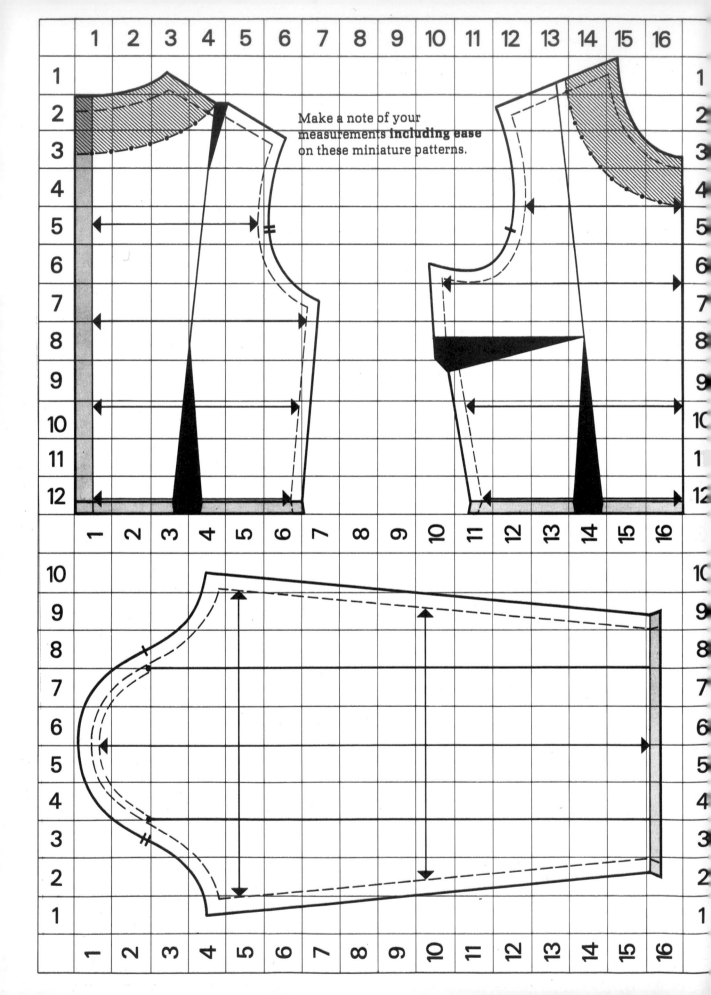

Make a note of your measurements **including ease** on these miniature patterns.

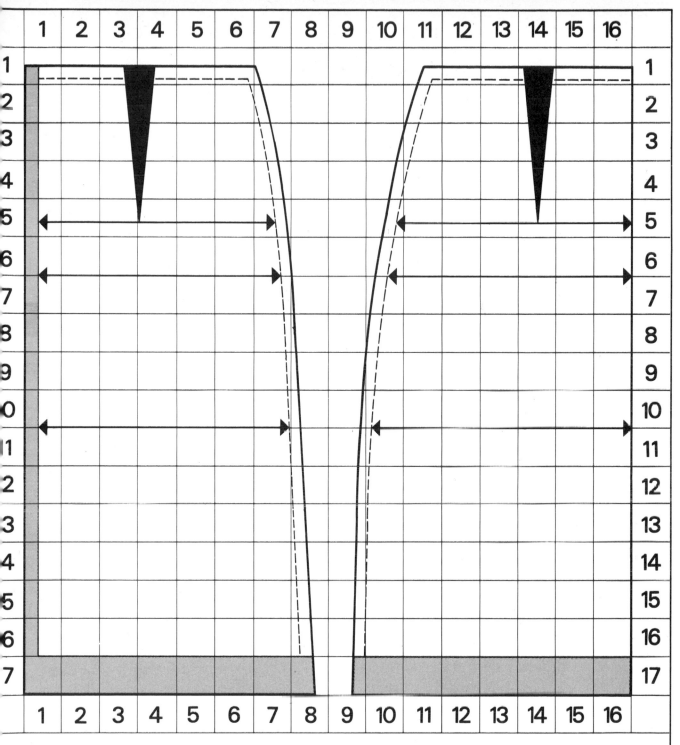

Fill in your measurements on the miniatures on pp 20 and 21 for reference. Trace off the miniatures to try out the ideas in the book.

Note that you can also copy these grids onto Betty Foster's Designer Paper which is available in girls' sizes 7-14 and women's sizes 10-22.

ADAPTING TO FASHION

CREATING FASHION PART 1: THE MASTER PATTERN AS A JIGSAW

There are many different ways of cutting up a picture to form a jigsaw puzzle. And your Master Pattern is exactly like a picture.

You can cut it on different lines and this creates new designs when you come to sew it back together again.

In a jigsaw puzzle the edges of each piece just touch one another. The edges of the pattern jigsaw must have a seam allowance added to them so that the cut edges can be sewn together. That is the only difference between the pattern and the jigsaw, and it is the first important thing you need to remember.

Whenever you cut up your Master Pattern, always mark the edges in red where you will need to make a seam. This will remind you to add a seam allowance.

Using the waistline

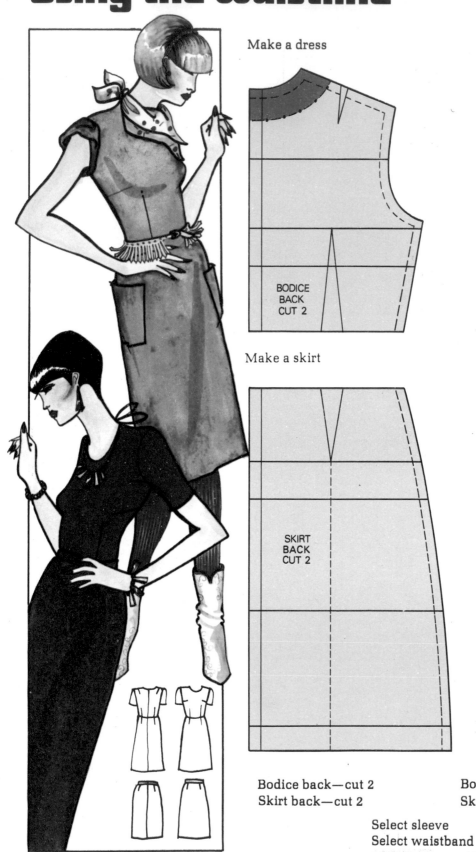

Make a dress

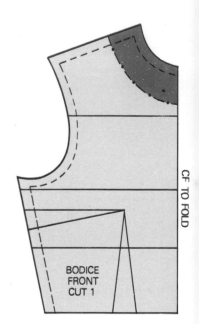

BODICE BACK CUT 2

BODICE FRONT CUT 1

CF TO FOLD

Make a skirt

SKIRT BACK CUT 2

FRONT SKIRT CUT 1

CF TO FOLD

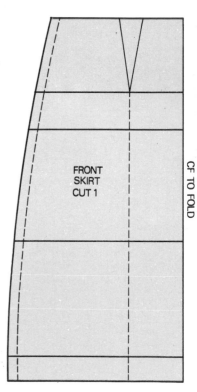

Bodice back—cut 2
Skirt back—cut 2

Bodice front—cut 1
Skirt front—cut 1

Select sleeve
Select waistband

Using the diaphragm line

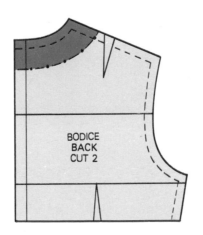

BODICE
BACK
CUT 2

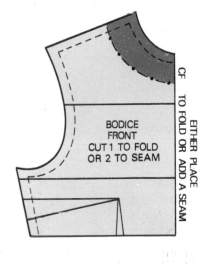

CF

TO FOLD OR ADD A SEAM

EITHER PLACE

BODICE
FRONT
CUT 1 TO FOLD
OR 2 TO SEAM

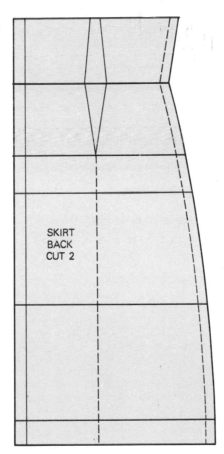

SKIRT
BACK
CUT 2

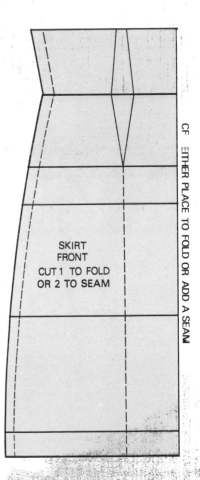

CF

EITHER PLACE TO FOLD OR ADD A SEAM

SKIRT
FRONT
CUT 1 TO FOLD
OR 2 TO SEAM

Back bodice—cut 2

Back dress—cut 2

Front bodice—cut 1 to fold
or 2 with seam

Front dress—cut 1 to fold
or 2 with seam

Using the yoke line

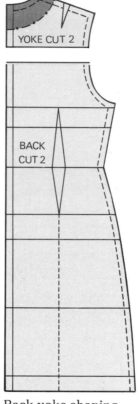

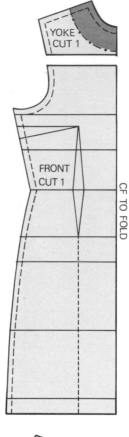

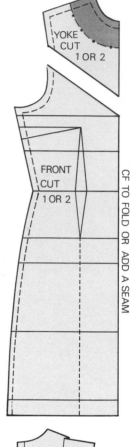

YOKE CUT 2

BACK CUT 2

YOKE CUT 1

FRONT CUT 1

CF TO FOLD

YOKE CUT 1 OR 2

FRONT CUT 1 OR 2

CF TO FOLD OR ADD A SEAM

Back yoke shaping

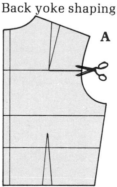

A

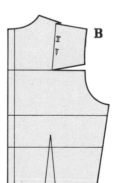

B

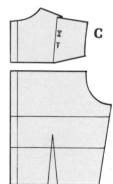

C

A Cut from armhole edge to where shoulder dart meets back line.
B Fold out the shoulder dart to produce a new dart at the armhole.
C Continue cutting across the back to complete the yoke.

Back yoke—cut 2
Front yoke—cut 1 to fold
    or 2 with seam

Back dress—cut 2
Front dress—cut 1 to fold
    or 2 with seam

Select sleeve

Changing the neckline

If you want to change the neckline you should use the chest and bust lines on the front pattern to help you select the right shape for the *front first*.

Draw in the new front neckline then place it to the back shoulder and draw the back neckline that you require.

Notice that in diagrams 1 and 2 the shoulder dart is retained, but with diagram 3—a much wider and lower neckline—the shoulder dart is no longer necessary.

Facings are cut from the main pattern outline following the neck shape.

1 Square neckline

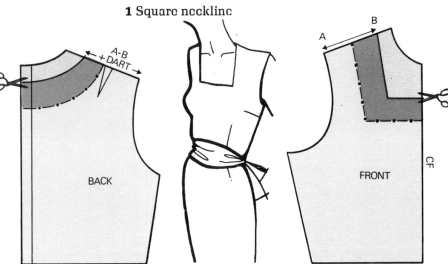

2 V-neckline
A centre front seam is recommended for this style.

3 Scoop neckline
Details of how to tighten lower necklines to avoid 'bagging' are given on p 6.

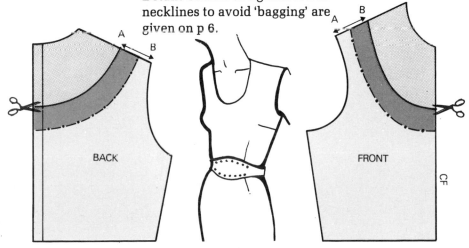

Using the hip line

You can always have the opening at the front instead of at the back. Simply put the centre back to the fold of the material and omit the seam allowance. Cut the front with a slightly larger seam allowance (recommended 2.5 cm/1 inch) or add a wrapover.

Back bodice—cut 1 (fold)
2 (seam)
Front bodice—cut 1 (fold)
2 (seam)
Back skirt—cut 1 (fold)
2 (seam)
Front skirt—cut 1 (fold)
2 (seam)

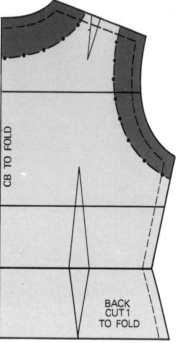

CB TO FOLD

BACK
CUT 1
TO FOLD

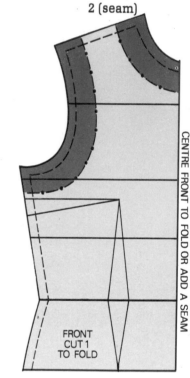

CENTRE FRONT TO FOLD OR ADD A SEAM

FRONT
CUT 1
TO FOLD

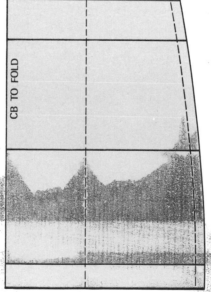

CB TO FOLD

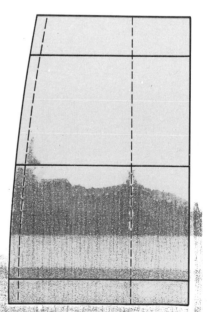

Adding a front fastening

To add a wrapover fastening to the centre front extend the pattern 4 cm (1¾ inches) over the centre line. (This includes the seam allowance.)

Position buttons and buttonholes to suit. It is best to start with the first button on the bustline and calculate the others from that point.

Facings are cut as indicated.

WAIST DARTS

This is a style where you can choose to leave the waist darts out when you sew up the garment.

You can then wear it unbelted or belted, to give a gentle gathered effect above and below the waist.

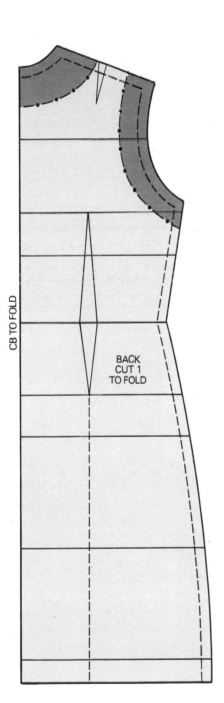

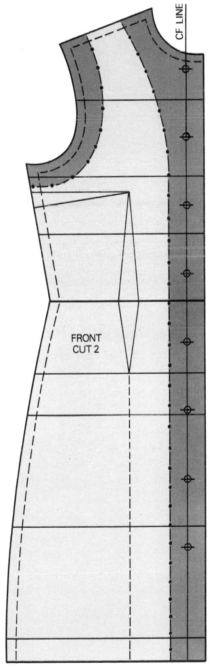

More wrapover ideas

ARMHOLES
Note: with sleeveless jackets the armhole should be lowered slightly as indicated.

NECKLINE
Adjust front and back necklines as indicated.

Fully line this waistcoat to avoid having to face the shaped hemline.

Fabric and lining (cut from the same pattern)

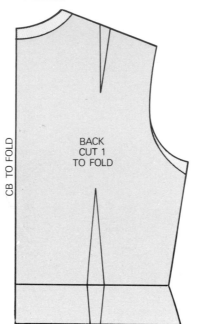

BACK
CUT 1
TO FOLD

CB TO FOLD

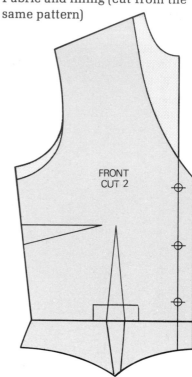

FRONT
CUT 2

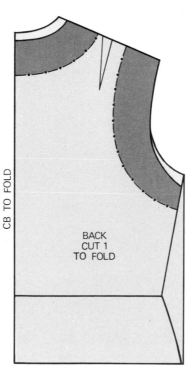

BACK
CUT 1
TO FOLD

CB TO FOLD

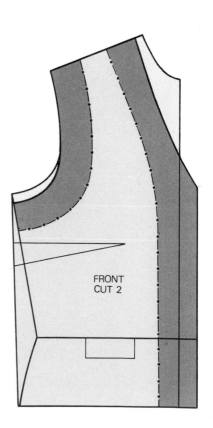

FRONT
CUT 2

Looking at skirts

On the Master Pattern dress there is a 5 cm (2 inch) fitting ease allowed at the waist. If you like to wear your skirts tighter at the waist you should adjust the waist before cutting out.
Either A Increase the size of the darts

or B Add an extra dart at each side front and back

or C Reduce sides of the skirt, front and back, grading down to the lower hip line.

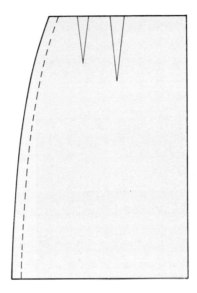

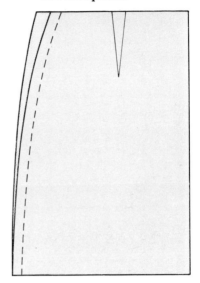

Waistbands
1 Iron on Vilene 'Fold-a-band' interfacing leaving seam allowance as indicated.

2 Fold fabric lengthwise and stitch the ends, clipping seam where stitching ends on top edge.

3 Turn band to right side and position skirt fastening.
Note this method can be used for cuffs and for bias-cut binding where tie ends are required.

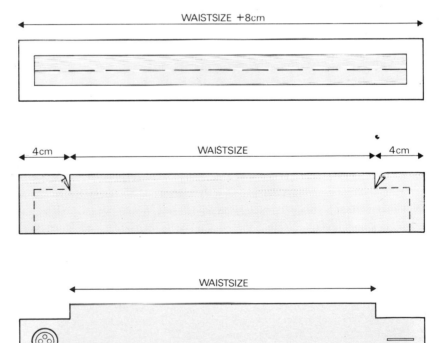

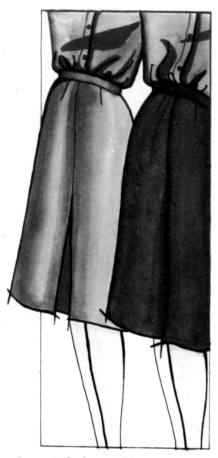

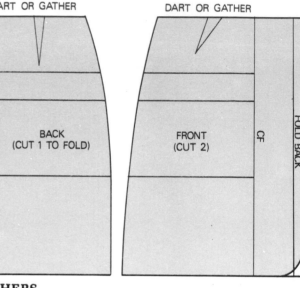

DARTS OR GATHERS

You can always replace the darts by gathers if you prefer. Both are merely a means of fitting the waistline to your body.

You can increase the darts for a closer fit, or make one dart into two, provided they take up only the amount of material required.

Inverted pleat Add 12 cm (4½ inches) to centre front.
Knife pleat Add 8 cm (3 inches) to centre front.

In each case place front pattern to fold.

(Instructions for making waistbands on p 31.)

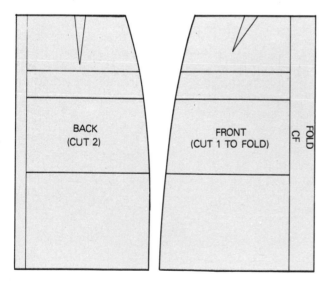

Simple trousers

Simple trousers from a corrected skirt pattern

1 Take your crutch measurement A-B-C.

Crutch measurement

2 Using the crutch conversion patterns select your nearest size. Cut out the pattern.
3 Place the crutch patterns onto the centre front and centre back lines of the skirt patterns.
4 Measure your outside leg and extend the pattern, adding a hem.

Outside leg measurement

5 Check your inside leg measurement.
6 The trouser legs can be tapered or flared as required.

To make an elasticated waist
Add a 5 cm (2 inch) hem to the top and turn over to form hem casing for the elastic.

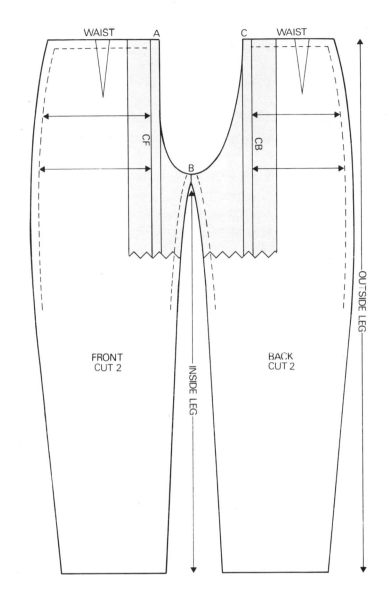

To add a fitted waistband
Raise the waist at the centre back by 1 cm (½ inch) and drop to natural waist at centre front.

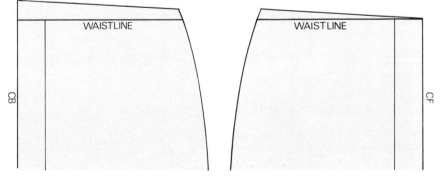

Using a correct trouser pattern to make a simple jumpsuit

Pin front and back bodice to front and back trouser pattern at the waistline, matching the darts.

Back—cut 2
Front—cut 2
Select collar
Select sleeve

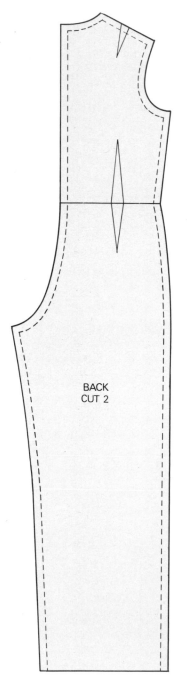

BACK
CUT 2

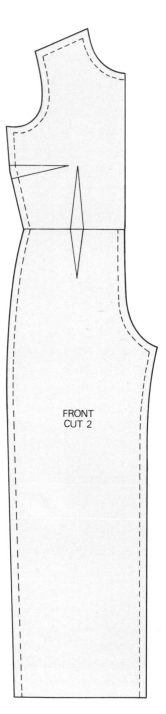

FRONT
CUT 2

Place the trouser back and front pattern together at the side seam. Add sufficient bodice pattern up to the underarm.
Elasticate top, waist and hems.
Cut straps on crossways fabric.

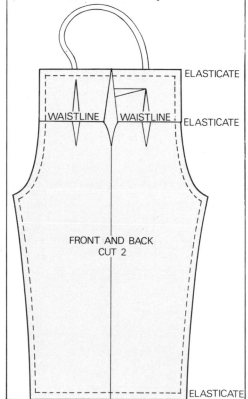

ELASTICATE

WAISTLINE   WAISTLINE

ELASTICATE

FRONT AND BACK
CUT 2

ELASTICATE

ADAPTING TO FASHION

CREATING FASHION PART 2: MOVING THE DARTS

The simple operation of moving the darts is perhaps the most exciting step in dress design.

The front bodice is shaped to accommodate the fullness of the bosom by the side bust dart. As long as the fullness is retained, the dart can be moved elsewhere to create a new line and a new shape. In other words, this dart is a major key to dress design.

You have already discovered that the waist darts in a dress can either be put in or left out depending on how you feel. Your dress can be loose or fitted. But the fullness made by the side bust dart can **never** be left out—it is always there because your pattern must always accommodate the bust. However, the dart itself can be moved into different positions and used to create different effects. As you will see, it may even seem to have vanished altogether.

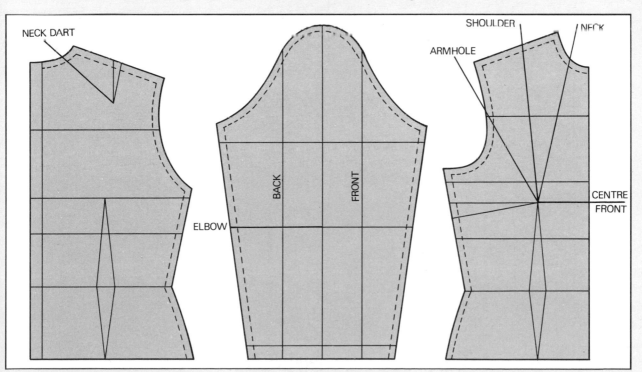

NECK DART

BACK

FRONT

ELBOW

SHOULDER

ARMHOLE

NECK

CENTRE FRONT

The shoulder dart

Draw a line down from the centre front shoulder to the point where the waist and bust darts meet. Cut down this line, stopping dead at the bust. Fold out the side bust dart, indicated by the pin in the diagram.

The shaping has now been moved to the shoulder, and if you cut the new shoulder line B-B, and stitch the new dart A-X-A, you will have identical shaping to the original pattern.

With the shaping in this new position you can now choose to use it either as gathers (diagram 1), tucks (diagram 2), or you can make a two-piece princess-line pattern following the instructions in diagram 3.

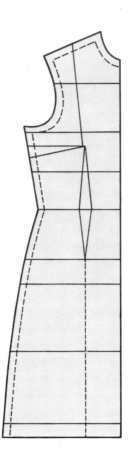

FRONT

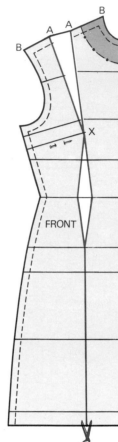

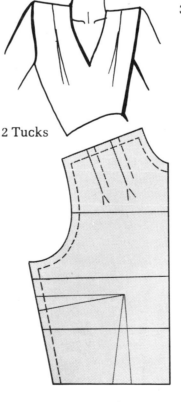

1 Gathers

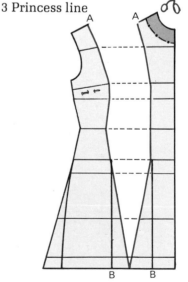

2 Tucks

3 Princess line

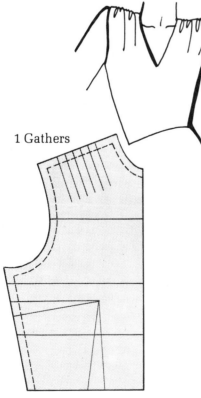

Note: waist dart is cut away to form shaping

The skirt can be flared by extending the seams from the first or second hipline.

The armhole dart

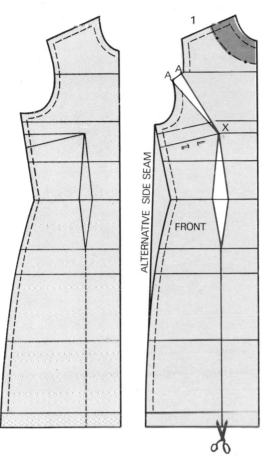

Draw a line from the armhole to the point where the waist and bust darts meet. Cut down this line to point X and close the side bust dart, indicated by a pin in the diagram.

In diagram 1 you can see this dart A-X-A can be stitched in, and the side seams flared in a new style. The waist darts are omitted.

In diagram 2 the front pattern has been cut in two for the princess line, and the waist shaping retained.

Note: cut armhole facings before dart is moved.

The bust shape at point X should be gently curved.

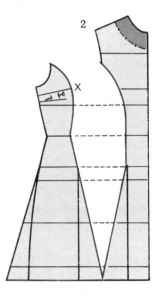

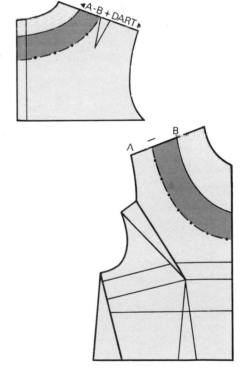

The neckline dart

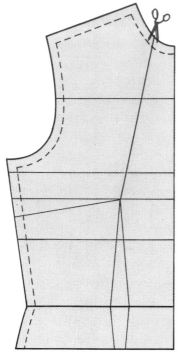

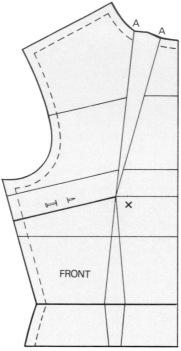

FRONT

Draw a line from the centre of the neckline to the point where the waist dart and the bust dart meet. Cut down this line to point X and close the side bust dart, indicated in the diagram with a pin.

The shaping has now moved to the neckline.

GATHERS INSTEAD OF DARTS

With the shaping coming from the neckline it is best to gather the distance A – A back to size.

This neckline is best in soft fabrics, and is usually finished with binding rather than with fastenings.

HALTER TOP
Ties or collar continued from neck binding

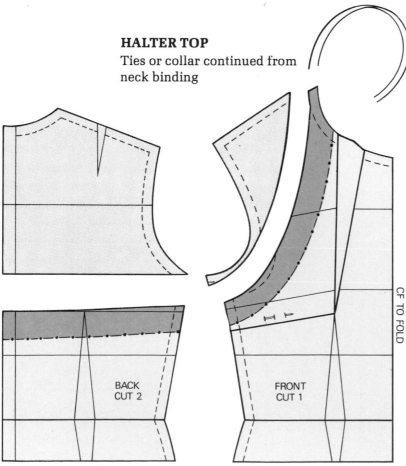

BACK
CUT 2

FRONT
CUT 1

CF TO FOLD

Hem shaping

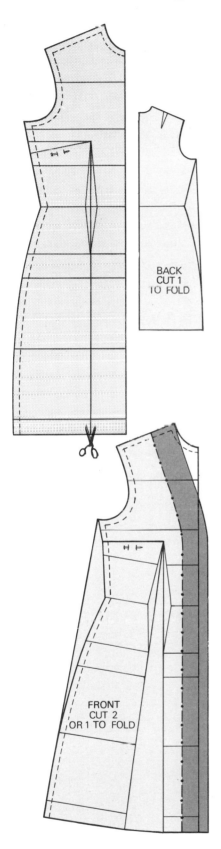

BACK
CUT 1
TO FOLD

FRONT
CUT 2
OR 1 TO FOLD

This is one of the occasions when you would have to look carefully at a design before you saw that the bust shaping was actually coming from the hemline.

The pattern is cut up from the hem to the bust point and the side dart is closed out. This produces the flared hemline, and if you try it out small-scale in fabric you will see that the front falls beautifully without any strain over the bust.

The back pattern is flared on the side seam as in the diagram. The centre front can be put to a fold, or you can add a wrap or a seam to the front edge.

For roll collar see p 64

More dart movements

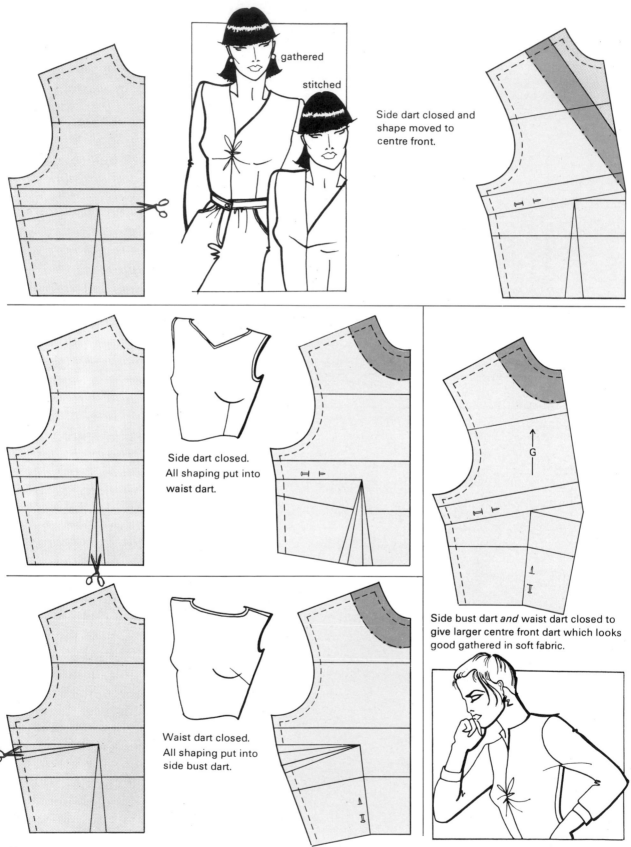

gathered

stitched

Side dart closed and shape moved to centre front.

Side dart closed. All shaping put into waist dart.

Side bust dart *and* waist dart closed to give larger centre front dart which looks good gathered in soft fabric.

Waist dart closed. All shaping put into side bust dart.

G

ADAPTING TO FASHION

THE BACK

For obvious reasons a large part of the dress designer's skill is involved in the front pattern. The back pattern is best altered and adapted after the front has been determined.

The back shoulder line must be corrected to match the front, and the design lines of the front should be considered when altering the back pattern.

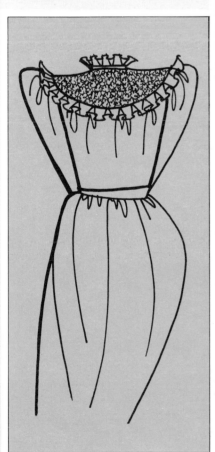

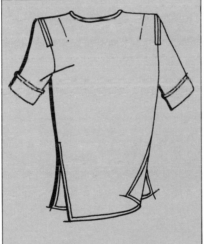

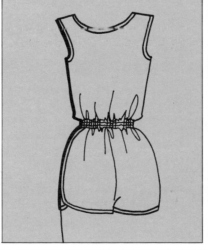

Neckline and shoulder dart

The shoulder dart can be moved into the neckline. This is particularly useful if a well-fitted back neckline is required.

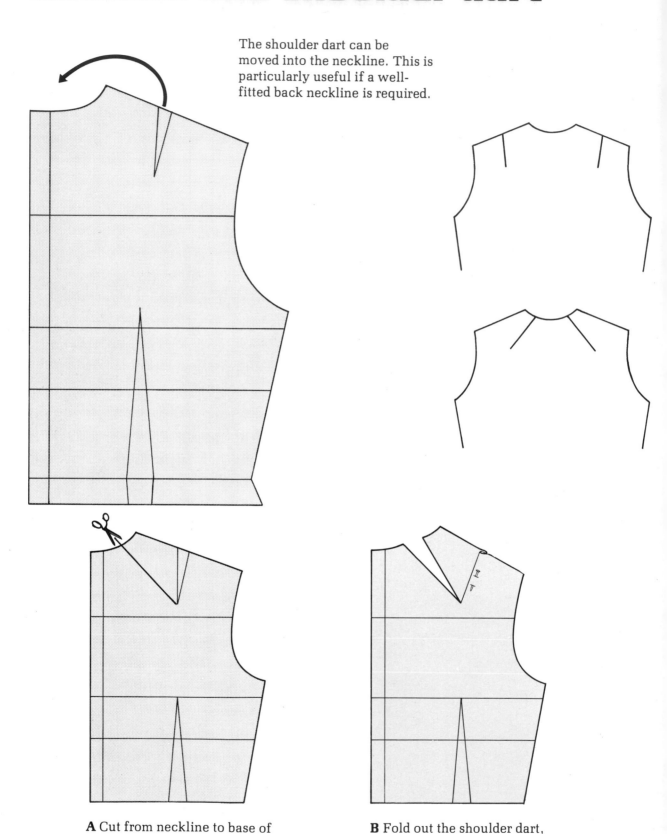

A Cut from neckline to base of dart.

B Fold out the shoulder dart, opening the neckline.

Princess line

The back pattern can be designed to correspond with the front detail. In this case it follows the princess line from p 36 and care should be taken to match the front and back seaming on the shoulder.

The back pattern is cut through taking out the shoulder and waist darts.

The centre back is kept on the straight.

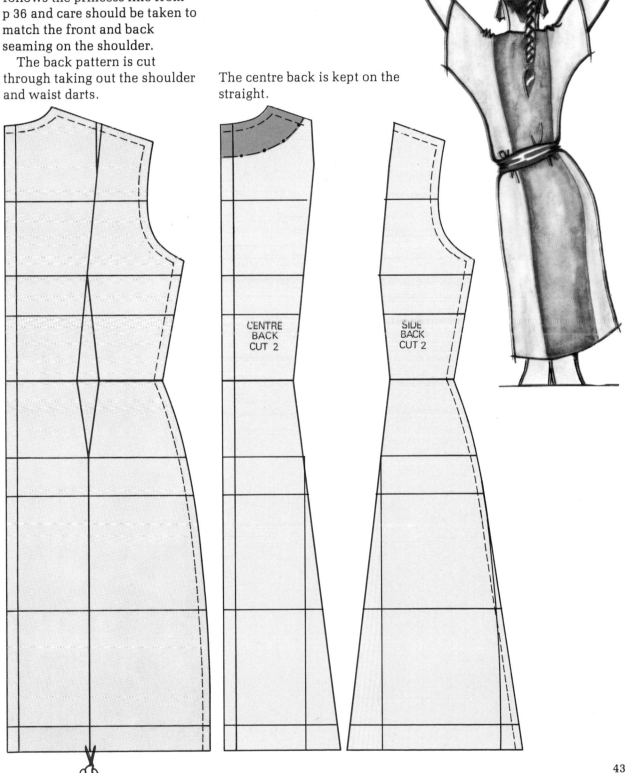

CENTRE
BACK
CUT 2

SIDE
BACK
CUT 2

Back shaped from armhole

The back pattern split from the armhole.

Flare can be added to the centre and side panels of the back.

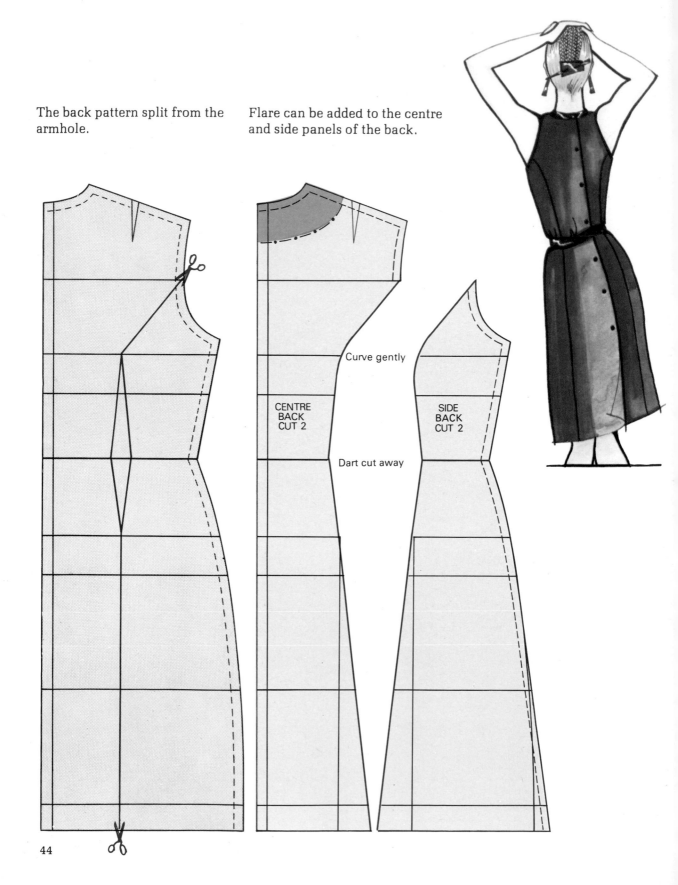

Curve gently

CENTRE
BACK
CUT 2

Dart cut away

SIDE
BACK
CUT 2

ADAPTING TO FASHION

SLEEVES AND COLLARS

Now that you know the rules about cutting the pattern, adding seam allowances, adding flare, and closing the darts to move their position, you will have no difficulty in reading the diagram instructions from here on.

Set-in sleeve

On the elbow line, cut from the back edge to the centre line. Close the dart out at the wrist to the required size. This will then open out the elbow dart.

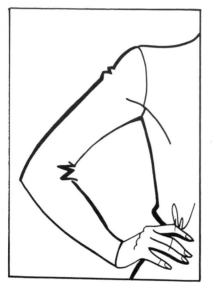

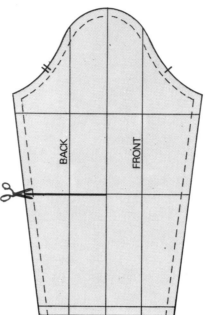

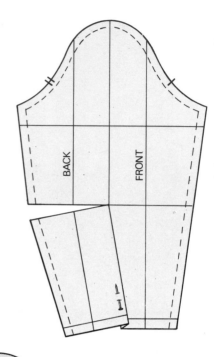

Flared sleeve

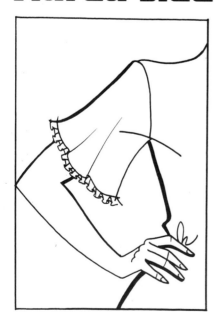

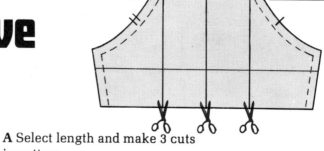

A Select length and make 3 cuts in pattern.

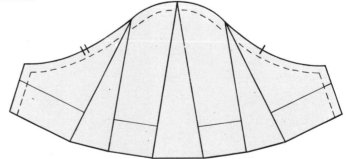

B Spread the bottom of the sleeve to required width. This is an ideal style for delicate fabrics.

Bishop sleeve

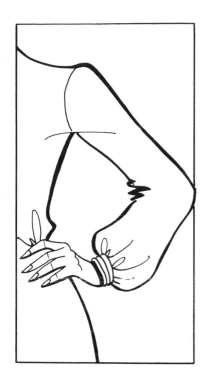

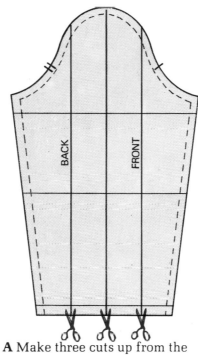

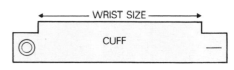

Cuff—cut 2

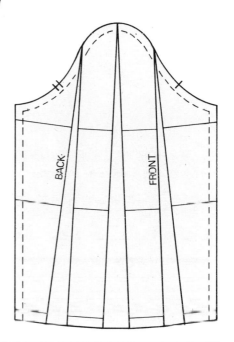

A Make three cuts up from the wrist.
B Spread sleeve to required width.

Puff sleeve

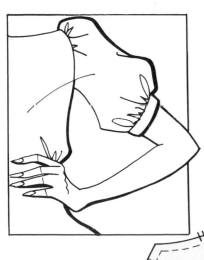

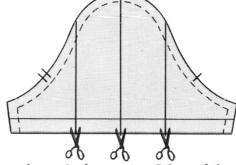

A Select length required.
B Make three cuts up from the bottom.

C Spread the pattern both at the head and at the bottom.
D Gather the head to the armhole size and gather the bottom to fit sleeve band or binding.

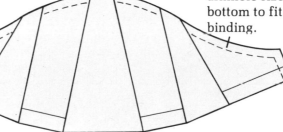

Shirt sleeve

Bell sleeve

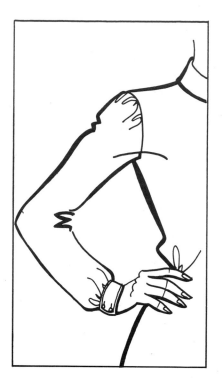

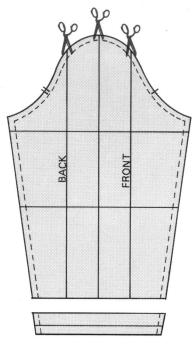

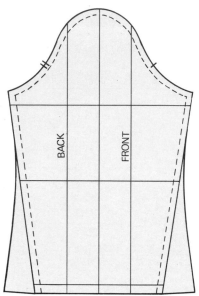

A Shorten sleeve pattern by about 3 cm (1¼ inches) to allow for cuff. Make three cuts from the hem to the sleeve head.

Shape the side seams outwards from the elbow line to the required width. Cut facing for sleeve bottom.

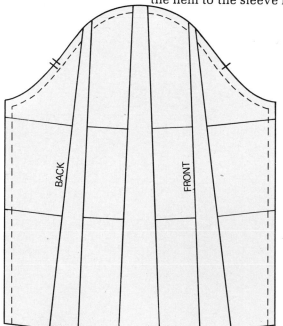

B Spread the pattern to produce straight sides, with a slightly increased gather at the head.

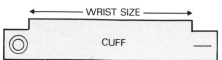

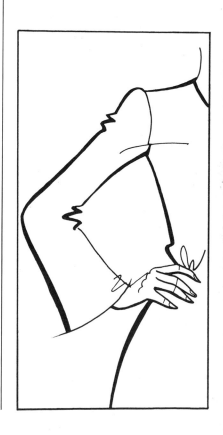

Peter Pan collar

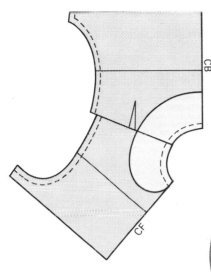

A Pin front and back shoulders together without closing back shoulder dart.
B Draw collar onto the neckline.
C This produces a flat collar pattern fitting the neck.

D To produce a collar which stands up at the back of the neck fold out small darts on the *outer* collar edge until the collar is practically straight.
E Add seam allowance to outer edge.

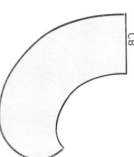

Shawl collar

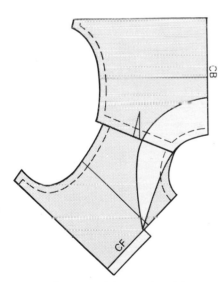

C This produces a flat collar pattern fitting the neck.

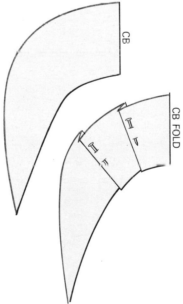

A Pin front and back shoulder without closing back shoulder dart. Draw in the neckline selected.
B Draw in the collar required.

D To produce a higher or 'stand' collar, fold out small darts at the back of the collar only.
E Add seam allowance to outer edge.

Simple collars by measurement

Straight collar

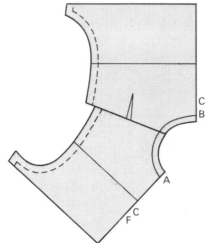

The straight collar is simply the neck measurement, cut to any width, with points added to the outer edge.

Remember to add the seam allowance to the outer edge.

Simple collars by measurement

Pin the front and back shoulders together with the neck edges level, and without pinning out the shoulder dart.

Accurately measure around the neck edge, on the stitching line, from A to B. This will give you *half* the collar size needed.

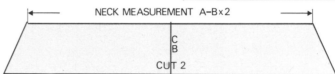

Collar—cut 2, either full length or with CB to fold.

Add seam to outer edge.

Mandarin collar

A For the mandarin collar the neck measurement is at the bottom edge. Select the width and curve the ends. Remember to add a seam allowance to the outer edges.

B To fit the neck small darts are folded out of the top edge to achieve the correct curved outline.

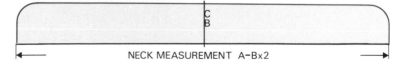

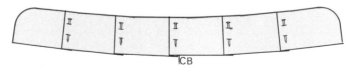

Tighten the top edge for a closer fit.

Collar—cut 2, either full length or with CB to fold.

Shirt collar

Pin shoulders together. Add wrap to front edge. Measure A-B on stitching line.

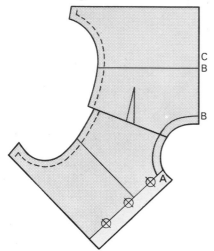

Neckline with wrap added for shirt collar.

Collar—cut 2, either full length or with CB to fold.
Add wrap allowance to each end and seam allowance to outer edge.

Note: this collar is stitched right to the edge of the wrap front.

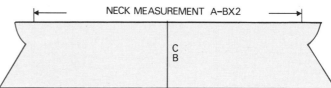

Roll collar

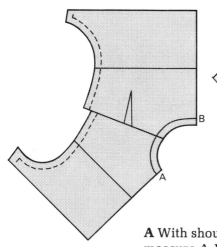

A With shoulders pinned measure A-B on the stitching line. Add seam allowance on *all* edges.
B Cut one collar on the cross of the fabric and fold on the centre line.

Care should be taken to cut the collar absolutely on the cross of the fabric.

ADAPTING TO FASHION

EASY DRESS DESIGN

If you have worked through the book to this stage you should now be ready to make your own clothes. Practise the patterns in miniature first, before transferring them to your Master Pattern. The pictures and sketches are designed to stimulate your imagination; when you are working in the small scale you will discover how the patterns were made.

Casual blouse

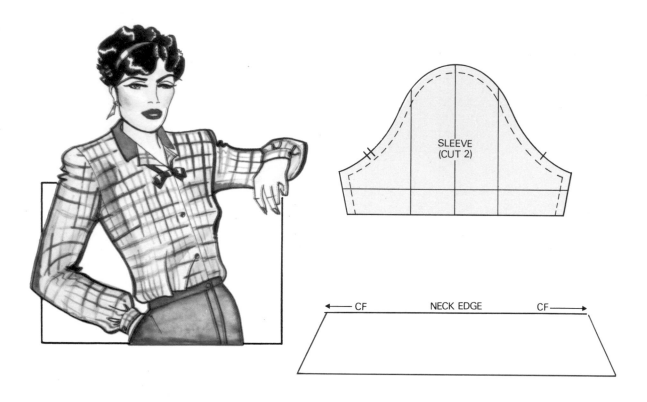

SLEEVE
(CUT 2)

CF ← NECK EDGE → CF

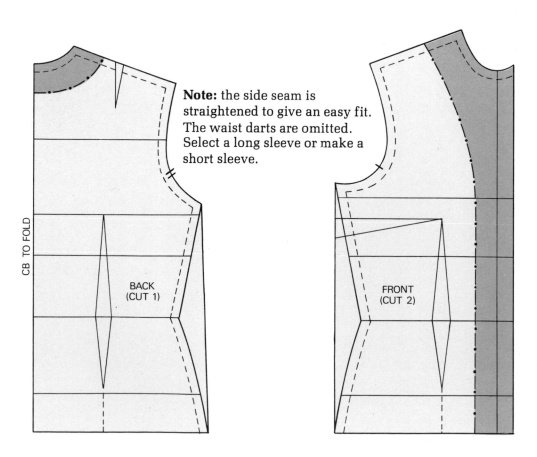

CB TO FOLD

BACK
(CUT 1)

Note: the side seam is straightened to give an easy fit. The waist darts are omitted. Select a long sleeve or make a short sleeve.

FRONT
(CUT 2)

Blouse with front and back yoke

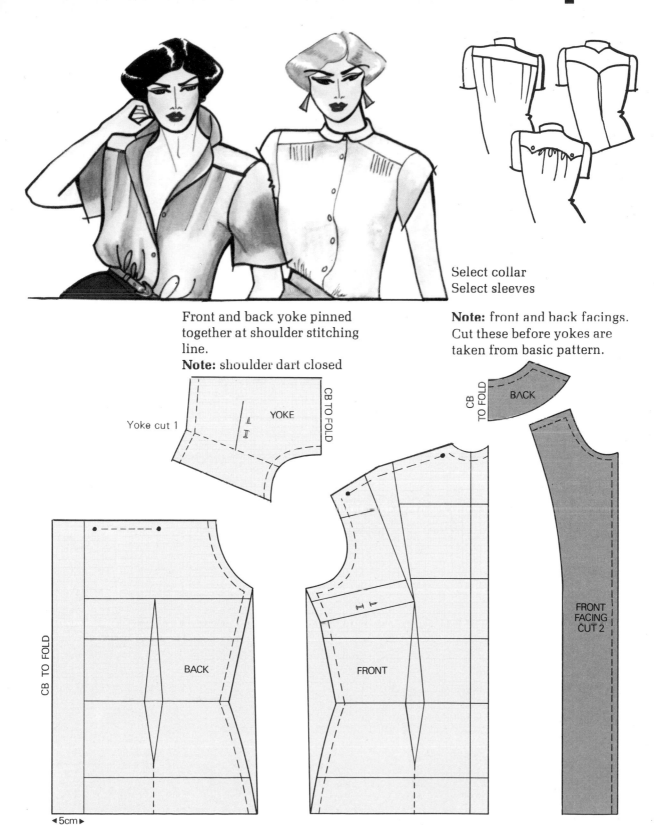

Select collar
Select sleeves

Front and back yoke pinned together at shoulder stitching line.
Note: shoulder dart closed

Note: front and back facings. Cut these before yokes are taken from basic pattern.

Yoke cut 1

YOKE

CB TO FOLD

CB TO FOLD

BACK

FRONT FACING CUT 2

CB TO FOLD

BACK

FRONT

◀5cm▶

Back—cut 1. Omit waist darts

Front—cut 2. Omit waist darts

Shirt or dress

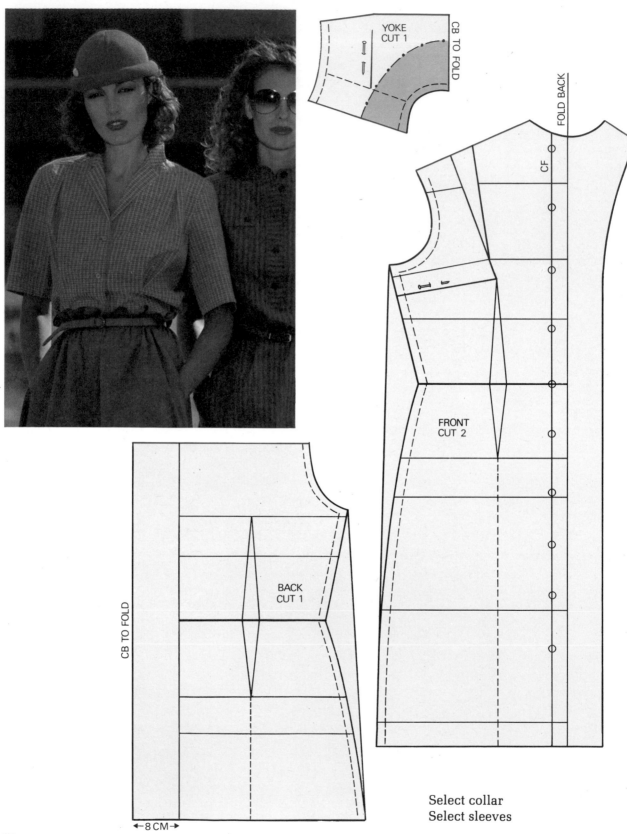

YOKE
CUT 1

CB TO FOLD

FOLD BACK

CF

FRONT
CUT 2

CB TO FOLD

BACK
CUT 1

←8 CM→

Select collar
Select sleeves

Skirt patterns on p 32

Skirts

Six-gore skirt

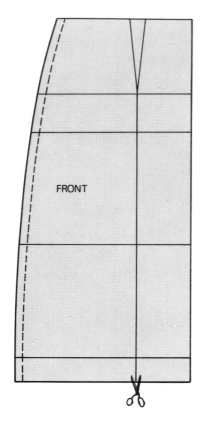

FRONT

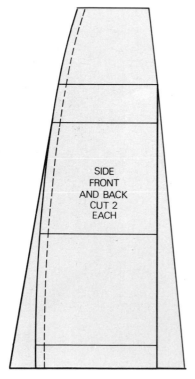

SIDE
FRONT
AND BACK
CUT 2
EACH

CENTRE
FRONT
AND BACK
CUT 1
EACH

CENTRE FRONT AND BACK TO FOLD

Close half the dart amount so that only a small dart remains   **Slightly flared skirt**

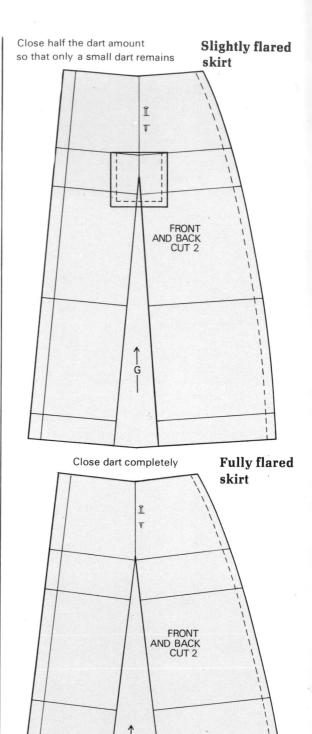

FRONT
AND BACK
CUT 2

G

Close dart completely   **Fully flared skirt**

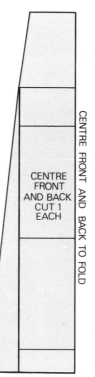

FRONT
AND BACK
CUT 2

G

Sleeve and Yoke in one

This design has the sleeve and the yoke cut in one piece.

1 Move the side bust dart into its new position over the bust point.

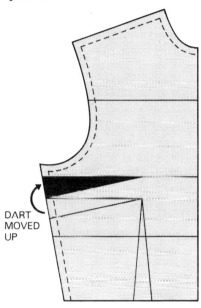

DART
MOVED
UP

2 Continue the shoulder line to the required sleeve length.

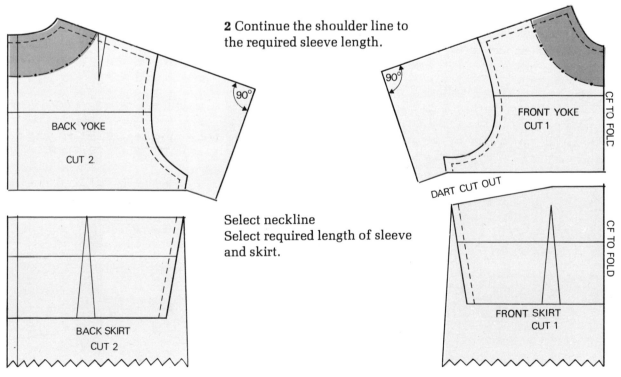

90°

BACK YOKE

CUT 2

90°

FRONT YOKE
CUT 1

CF TO FOLD

DART CUT OUT

Select neckline
Select required length of sleeve and skirt.

BACK SKIRT
CUT 2

FRONT SKIRT
CUT 1

CF TO FOLD

Smock dress

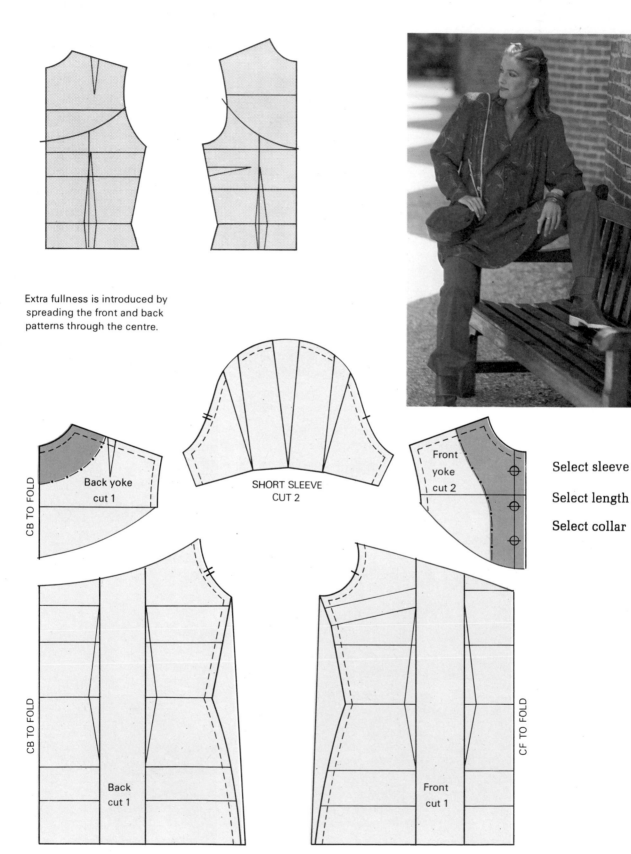

Extra fullness is introduced by spreading the front and back patterns through the centre.

CB TO FOLD

Back yoke
cut 1

SHORT SLEEVE
CUT 2

Front
yoke
cut 2

Select sleeve

Select length

Select collar

CB TO FOLD

Back
cut 1

Front
cut 1

CF TO FOLD

Overdress with lined bodice

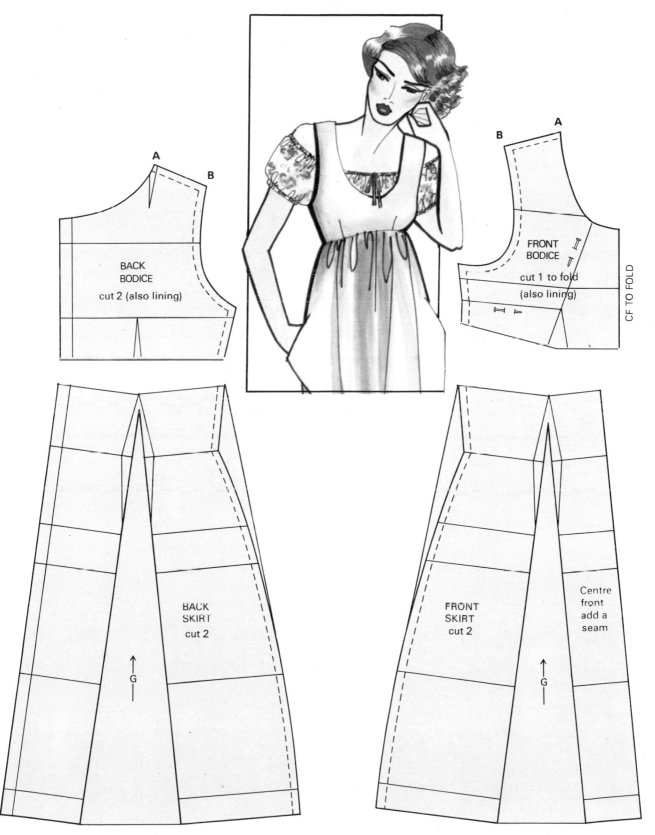

A

B

BACK
BODICE
cut 2 (also lining)

B

A

FRONT
BODICE
cut 1 to fold
(also lining)

CF TO FOLD

BACK
SKIRT
cut 2

G

FRONT
SKIRT
cut 2

Centre
front
add a
seam

G

H-line dress with bound neckline

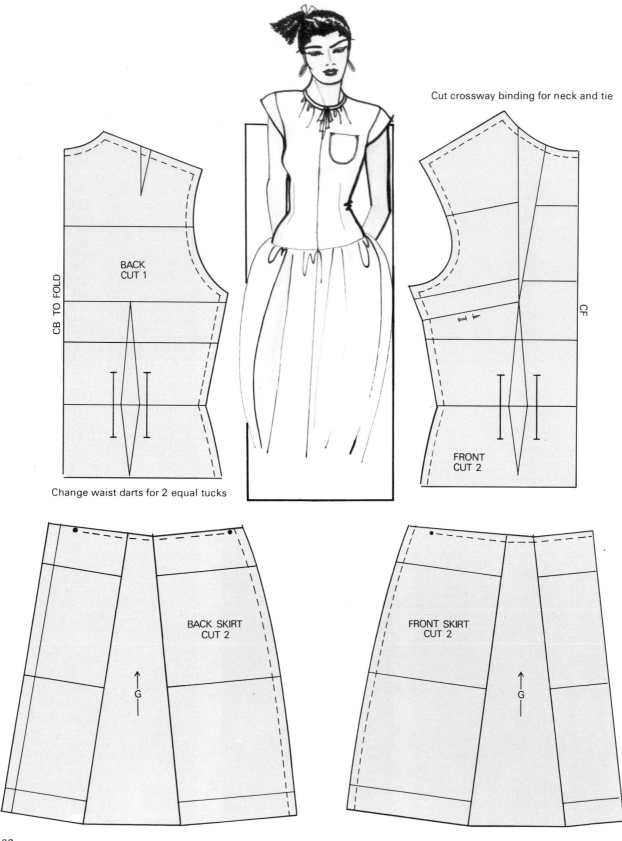

Cut crossway binding for neck and tie

CB TO FOLD

BACK
CUT 1

CF

FRONT
CUT 2

Change waist darts for 2 equal tucks

BACK SKIRT
CUT 2

G

FRONT SKIRT
CUT 2

G

Single-breasted jacket

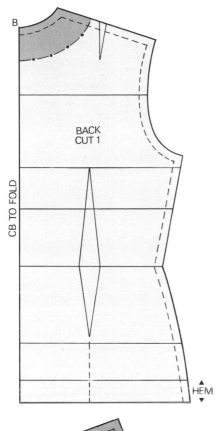

BACK
CUT 1

CB TO FOLD

HEM

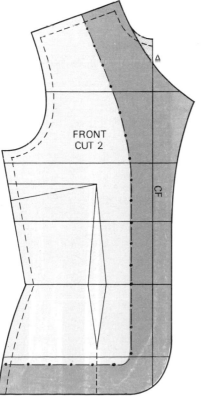

FRONT
CUT 2

CF

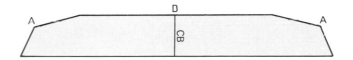

A   D   A

CB

Make collar length A-B when shoulders are pinned together. Shape ends of collar slightly. **Note:** front requires hem facing. Back requires hem.

Collar—cut 2
Select sleeve

Roll-collar jacket

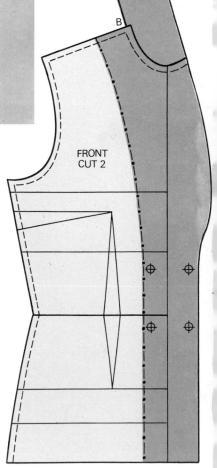

Back—cut 1 to fold
Front—cut 2
Front facing (which also
includes back collar facing)—
cut 2

Select sleeve